WHAT'S LOST

by Paula B Stanic

Copyright © 2021 by Paula B Stanic
All Rights Reserved

WHAT'S LOST is fully protected under the copyright laws of the British Commonwealth, including Canada, the United States of America, and all other countries of the Copyright Union. All rights, including professional and amateur stage productions, recitation, lecturing, public reading, motion picture, radio broadcasting, television, online/digital production, and the rights of translation into foreign languages are strictly reserved.

ISBN 978-0-573-13261-2

concordtheatricals.co.uk
concordtheatricals.com

FOR PRODUCTION ENQUIRIES
UNITED KINGDOM AND WORLD
EXCLUDING NORTH AMERICA
licensing@concordtheatricals.co.uk
020-7054-7298

NORTH AMERICA
info@concordtheatricals.com
1-866-979-0447

Each title is subject to availability from Concord Theatricals, depending upon country of performance.

CAUTION: Professional and amateur producers are hereby warned that *WHAT'S LOST* is subject to a licensing fee. The purchase, renting, lending or use of this book does not constitute a license to perform this title(s), which license must be obtained from the appropriate agent prior to any performance. Performance of this title(s) without a license is a violation of copyright law and may subject the producer and/or presenter of such performances to penalties. Both amateurs and professionals considering a production are strongly advised to apply to the appropriate agent before starting rehearsals, advertising, or booking a theatre. A licensing fee must be paid whether the title is presented for charity or gain and whether or not admission is charged.

This work is published by Samuel French, an imprint of Concord Theatricals. Ltd

The Professional Rights in this play are controlled by Concord Theatricals, Aldwych House, 71-91 Aldwych, London, WC2B 4HN, UK.

No one shall make any changes in this title for the purpose of production. No part of this book may be reproduced, stored in a retrieval system, scanned, uploaded, or transmitted in any form, by any means, now known or yet to be invented, including mechanical, electronic, digital, photocopying, recording, videotaping, or otherwise, without the prior written permission of the publisher. No one shall share this title, or part of this title, to any social media or file hosting websites.

The moral right of Paula B Stanic to be identified as author of this work has been asserted in accordance with Section 77 of the Copyright, Designs and Patents Act 1988.

USE OF COPYRIGHTED MUSIC

A licence issued by Concord Theatricals to perform this play does not include permission to use the incidental music specified in this publication. In the United Kingdom: Where the place of performance is already licensed by the PERFORMING RIGHT SOCIETY (PRS) a return of the music used must be made to them. If the place of performance is not so licensed then application should be made to PRS for Music (www.prsformusic.com). A separate and additional licence from PHONOGRAPHIC PERFORMANCE LTD (www.ppluk.com) may be needed whenever commercial recordings are used. Outside the United Kingdom: Please contact the appropriate music licensing authority in your territory for the rights to any incidental music.

USE OF COPYRIGHTED THIRD-PARTY MATERIALS

Licensees are solely responsible for obtaining formal written permission from copyright owners to use copyrighted third-party materials (e.g., artworks, logos) in the performance of this play and are strongly cautioned to do so. If no such permission is obtained by the licensee, then the licensee must use only original materials that the licensee owns and controls. Licensees are solely responsible and liable for clearances of all third-party copyrighted materials, and shall indemnify the copyright owners of the play(s) and their licensing agent, Concord Theatricals Ltd., against any costs, expenses, losses and liabilities arising from the use of such copyrighted third-party materials by licensees.

IMPORTANT BILLING AND CREDIT REQUIREMENTS

If you have obtained performance rights to this title, please refer to your licensing agreement for important billing and credit requirements.

CHARACTERS

GINA – 43, Black British
RUDI – 17, (Debra & Lenny's daughter Rudene)
DEBRA – 41, (Gina's sister) Black British
LENNY – 41, White British
ALEX – 23, Black British

SETTING

A modern, minimal London home (inside and out). A park (where the remembrance is held). A hospital room and outside the hospital.

TIME

Originally set in 2008 but can be set later.

AUTHOR'S NOTES

Though they are distinct there is something of Debra and Gina in each other. The actresses playing them could alternate in each performance.

FILMED/ RECORDED NEWS FLASHES

Recorded flashes from three news reporters or/ and images of news feeds can be projected through the space. Companies may create their own version using the content of those that appear in this script.

NOTES ON TEXT

/ indicates next line comes straight in.

… indicates the character's struggle for a word, thought or response.

The song in scene 1 is something Gina and Rudi danced to when Rudi was much younger. It can be chosen by the actresses.

Full stops at the end of lines are sometimes omitted if the character's not quite finished, despite having stopped talking.

NOTES ON STAGING

We should be able to see inside and outside at the same time, so we move easily from one scene to another.

MASSIVE THANKS TO

All at The Alfred Fagon Award and the late Roland Rees. The brilliant creatives involved in readings/development: The Royal Court, Jo Martin, Tanya Moodie, Gary Carr, Suzie McGrath, Steve Hansell and Natalie Ibu. The Bush, Sarah Niles, Lorna French, Sean O'Callaghan, Ivan Oyik, Tia Bannon, Daniel Bailey, Darius McFarlane, Deirdre O'Halloran and Ifrah Ismail. James Bosely & Up Theater, NYC. Big thanks: Lisa Goldman, Nina Steiger, Brian Walters and Gareth Machin for support that's kept me writing. All at Concord Theatricals, particularly Charlie and Steven for the brilliant lockdown chat, also to Elliot Robinson at Playdead for always pushing and backing the play.

To: Karen Bardowell, Derek A Bardowell, Bev Issacs and good friends who inspired many parts. My fantastic nieces, nephew an family near and wide. Del, Youth Advocates, Activists & Mentors everywhere.

For
Elle, Pa & Fedj for just about everything.

1.

A Memory

*(**RUDI**'s room. 17-year-old **RUDI**, intelligent and intense speaks to **GINA**, 43, as they share a spliff. **GINA**'s head hangs between her legs.)*

RUDI. So these three... well, kids, just kids. They walk into Urban Outfitters. And everyone looks, cos they're... loud, really and you know, there's something, they don't look... Can't be more than twelve, thirteen. But they're wearing, you know, not the usual reality star on a budget gear. Bits but they've not got it. Wouldn't look if you couldn't hear them. Wouldn't notice...

*(**GINA** takes a deep breath.)*

Drugs, too many drugs, maybe.

GINA. Yeah, I can't take what I used to.

Much as I try.

*(**GINA** sits up, she's glamorous in her unique way, but also a bit of a mess.)*

RUDI. The second they step in, you know it, know some... collision's coming. Security man's on them. They just stare him out. Blank, blank looks. Make a show of picking things up, carrying them about, chucking them. You know, you see, feel but you can't... what can you, you just... watch.

*(**RUDI** stops and thinks.)*

Go downstairs, try to get into another space but, you know, I'm just listening out. Wandering by racks and rails of glittering outfits, through bags and hats, all this useless, useless stuff that means nothing. Cos something's going to kick off and... where will we all be after?

>   (**GINA** *takes a long, deep drag. She watches the smoke disintegrate in the air.*)

Start to think it's one of those imagined moments, except it's that... quiet as I start back up the stairs, that weird "it's waiting" quiet.

GINA. What's that?

RUDI. As I get closer to the top I feel the change, smell the panic. This... thing we'd all been waiting for has past. Past us, not him. See the face of the security guy who winked at me as I came in. He's collapsed on the floor with this face... his arm's turned the wrong way, all... out of line with his body. People crowd. We're all just there, present. And I don't want to be one of them, gathered, staring, involved, now it's all over.

So I walk

GINA. That's fucking awful.

RUDI. Sound rises behind me, sort of respectful. Everyone working together, now danger's gone. Disaster's passed and hasn't taken any of them. But he's lying there, maybe dead, maybe. For taking his job seriously or too seriously or just for doing it. He's lying there all collapsed, bent for trying to protect, what? And we're cowards or clever. Them, what did they get? And how are they so... convinced of their right to it that they knock out whatever's in their way?

GINA. Shop down Spitalfields. You know who's who in Spitalfields.

RUDI. See these moments everywhere. Not confined to Camden or Hackney.

GINA. Hackney's come up hasn't it?

RUDI. You know what I'm saying.

GINA. Yeah. World's got scarier.

RUDI. Just made me think…

(**RUDI** *glances at her.*)

Thought maybe I'd volunteer on this youth project? Help out with these workshops they have or something, but/

GINA. Great.

RUDI. Mum/

GINA. She'll come round/

RUDI. She expects/

GINA. Never mind others expectations/

RUDI. How do I do that?

GINA. Just go for it/

RUDI. She says I should focus.

(**GINA** *smiles to herself.*)

GINA. Focus.

RUDI. Says I'm too young to help other youth.

GINA. You need to do what's in your head.

RUDI. Told me I need to concentrate.

GINA. Take a few years out.

RUDI. Few years head down she says.

GINA. Don't wanna be one of those who never move outside their usual existence. How many trillions of miles is the planet? Don't feel it here, move on, that's what we're meant for.

RUDI. Yeah.

GINA. Staying in one place isn't normal. Dee should get that. Our parents did.

RUDI. ... Sometimes I just sit working it all through. What do you do?

GINA. What you can.

RUDI. Maybe.

> (**RUDI** *scans her mobile.*)

GINA. What time is it?

RUDI. Don't worry.

> (**GINA** *smiles at her.*)

GINA. What you doing here with me? Should be out with your mates.

RUDI. You're a mate, sort of.

GINA. Two years older than your mother.

RUDI. So?

GINA. Leather me if she walks in.

RUDI. Told you she won't.

GINA. Always pops up, pops out to catch me doing the wrong thing. Be struck off for this.

RUDI. She's working late.

GINA. Probably receives messages via satellite.

RUDI. She doesn't need technology.

> (*They smile together.*)

GINA. Lenny about?

RUDI. He's fine, smokes himself.

GINA. ... Yeah?

RUDI. Found a bag in his pocket once.

GINA. Won't stop the moralist breaking out if he catches you smoking though.

RUDI. He understands stress.

GINA. Stress now is it?

> (**RUDI** *gives her a look.*)

RUDI. I do it all the time.

She walked in once. Smelt it. Just said it was incense.

> (**GINA** *laughs to herself.*)

Meditative herbal incense. Should've just been honest.

GINA. Where would that get you?

RUDI. I'm nearly eighteen, I can take it.

> (**RUDI** *finds a track on her mobile.*)

Here's an old one for you.

> (*She plays a catchy hip-hop/R&B song.** *She mumbles the words looking at* **GINA**, *gets up and moves to it.*)

Come, do it with me.

> (**GINA** *just laughs, remembers.*)

You seriously not getting up?

> (**GINA** *watches* **RUDI**, *full of life, going for it, completely exaggerating their old, made up choreographed moves to the song.*)

---

* A licence to produce WHAT'S LOST does not include a performance licence for any third-party or copyrighted music. Licensees should create an original composition or use music in the public domain. For further information, please see Music Use Note on page iii.

Not as good without you.

(**RUDI** *leaves it, slumps down.*)

GINA. How d'you remember the dance?

RUDI. You always tell me about it.

GINA. Can't believe how time's just... gone.

(**GINA** *looks at her for a moment.*)

You don't, do you, smoke all the time?

RUDI. Don't try to be mum.

GINA. Just trying to be a decent aunty, once.

(**RUDI** *stares at* **GINA.**)

What?

RUDI. Nothing.

(*Silence, then* **RUDI** *finally says it.*)

Maybe... I could stay in Hastings with you for a bit?

GINA. She'd freak

RUDI. ...

GINA. Haven't you got things to sort here, college, all that stuff?

RUDI. All done.

GINA. Well yeah, maybe

RUDI. Really?

GINA. ... Yeah, in a couple of weeks or something.

RUDI. That'd be great.

GINA. Give me time to get back and sorted.

RUDI. Two of us on the beach, looking out at the sea at night.

GINA. Barely go down anymore.

RUDI. It'll be brilliant.

GINA. Went down a few months back, looked out it was murky. Leaden. Full of floating crap. Cans, paper, cigarette butt type shit. Who throws fag ends in the sea?

> (**RUDI** *watches* **GINA** *absently let ash from her spliff fall on the floor.* **RUDI** *smiles.*)

Yeah. Come, come up.

RUDI. Next week?

GINA. Date.

> (**RUDI** *does her own little celebration.*)

RUDI. Need some time to work out what I'll do.

GINA. Thought you said you were sorted.

> (**RUDI** *looks at her.*)

RUDI. I'm thinking again about Uni. Think I need to be out in the the world.

GINA. Ah

RUDI. You get it don't you?

GINA. Dee might not be so off point on the college thing. Though I say it for totally different reasons. It'll be good fun.

RUDI. But the world's in crisis

GINA. And it'll still be in it when you get out believe me

RUDI. I just think maybe… I should be out here with others trying to do something.

GINA. That's what student unions are for. Though you don't wanna use up all your going out energy taking them too seriously.

RUDI. I get stressed, thinking about everything, so much needs to change and not enough people seem to want to do anything different. They talk, they see and… complain, but they don't want to change themselves. I was speaking to this guy Alex at the project? He says some of the same stuff I think about. Why am I spending more years studying stuff when there's so much going on in the streets and people need help. There's a danger whole parts of our world could disappear and, it's real. I mean what use will exam results be if there's no world to get on with them in? What would I really be doing? Isn't it just… stupid carrying on in this… old way when It doesn't work like it anymore? I could get involved in, in some campaigns Alex says. Could volunteer abroad even, help build homes instead of sitting in a classroom talking. I could do something that really matters/

GINA. A bloke is it?

RUDI. It's not about him.

> (**GINA** *winks at her.*)

It's not.

GINA. Yeah alright.

RUDI. … Most of the time I think I'll never find a face… attractive enough to kiss.

GINA. Relax hon

> (**GINA** *gives her a big kiss on the head.*)

You will.

> (*The room falls apart.*)

2.

Dee and G

(**RUDI**'s room – one year on. Some debris from the fallout lies around. **GINA** stands clinging to a rucksack. She has a large, rolled up canvas under one arm. **DEBRA**, 41, sharp and efficient in dress and manner stands behind her. **GINA** is uneasy in **DEBRA**'s presence.)

DEBRA. You can put your things down.

(**GINA** doesn't, she just peeps round the room.)

I'll get you some bedding.

GINA. Don't go.

DEBRA. I'll be a minute.

GINA. I see her

DEBRA ...

GINA. When I sleep, sometimes when I'm by the castle or watching TV. Sometimes there'll be a, a shooting in something and I just/

DEBRA She wasn't shot.

GINA. I know/

DEBRA. It wasn't a gun.

GINA. No/

DEBRA. Nothing to do with all that.

GINA. Just... what I see/

DEBRA. Not a gangsta moment like people want to imagine.

GINA. ...

DEBRA. Just a pathetic little knife in the hands of a stupid child.

GINA. I know Dee/

DEBRA. Then why do you insist on seeing different?

GINA. That's not/

DEBRA. Turning it into some myth

GINA. No/

DEBRA. No?

GINA. Just... what goes round my head.

DEBRA. Should get it checked.

GINA. It's normal/

DEBRA. Strange/

GINA. Considering...

DEBRA. Considering.

>   (GINA *faces* DEBRA. *They stare at each other. Neither wants to break it, until* GINA *has to.* GINA *puts her things down. She fiddles awkwardly with her rucksack, gets out a small tube of hand cream and quietly creams her hands.*)

GINA. It's good to see you. Really, really good.

DEBRA. Yes.

GINA. You've lost weight.

>   (DEBRA *tuts.*)

What?

DEBRA. ... Everyone thinks it's fine to comment on my appearance.

GINA. Not seen you that's all.

(Silence.)

DEBRA. How come?

GINA. What?

DEBRA. You came, now

GINA. I/

DEBRA. Nothing going on in Hastings?

GINA. Hasting's is over.

DEBRA. Right.

GINA. Anyone there with imagination moves on after a couple of years.

DEBRA. You wanted somewhere, real.

GINA. It was what I could afford

DEBRA. I said you should choose Brighton

GINA. Don't need to follow everyone else

DEBRA. There's a reason people followed.

GINA. …

DEBRA. And your art?

GINA. Having a break… holiday.

DEBRA. Won't be the next Chris Ofili then?

GINA. I'm an animator

DEBRA. … Disney?

(GINA decides to be gentle.)

GINA. Don't pretend you don't understand what I do.

(Silence.)

DEBRA. So/

GINA. You stripped the room.

DEBRA. Almost a year.

GINA. A year

DEBRA. Longest

GINA. Yeah

>*(Silence.)*

Sorry/

DEBRA. How long do you want to stay?

GINA. I'm not sure

DEBRA. Do you need money?

GINA. …

DEBRA. The artist's life.

GINA. Thinking of moving back.

DEBRA. Here?

GINA. Thinking

DEBRA. Permanently?

GINA. See how it feels.

DEBRA. Expensive.

GINA. Everywhere's going that way.

DEBRA. Most of us are trying to get out.

GINA. Everywhere's going the same.

DEBRA. Is it?

GINA. … Just need a place, space for a week, two.

DEBRA. Yes.

GINA. And, to be here for a bit, with you an' Lenny. Where is he, work?

DEBRA. Away.

GINA. Away?

DEBRA. Yes.

    (**GINA** *stares at her a moment.*)

GINA. I'm sorry/

DEBRA. What would you do with the flat?

If you, escape.

    (*Silence.*)

GINA. I need… change.

DEBRA. Yes, I need a bit of that.

GINA. Thinking about a few things

DEBRA. Nice for you.

GINA. Thought about going off somewhere Cuba, Mexico somewhere… warm, with bright colours.

DEBRA. Right.

GINA. Just a thought

DEBRA. It's good. I would. If there was the chance.

Escape.

GINA. Come.

    (**DEBRA** *smiles at her.*)

We could do a road trip.

DEBRA. Do people really do those?

GINA. Dee and G out on the road.

DEBRA. I can't

GINA. You've never just taken off.

DEBRA. I have no time.

GINA. Take some.

DEBRA. I have a lot on.

GINA. It'll help

DEBRA. Really?

GINA. Just try it out, come with me and see.

DEBRA. No.

(A moment.)

Be okay in here tonight?

*(**GINA** looks around the room.)*

GINA. Next door'll do. Settee's fine.

DEBRA. I'm up late, some nights

GINA. Me too.

DEBRA. Most nights.

GINA. Sit up together, watch some late night crap.

DEBRA. I have people coming over, to help with, with this thing I'm planning. I'm not sure what time we'll finish.

GINA. … Probably be out late anyway. Catch up with a few people, see what's happening.

DEBRA. So in here is okay?

GINA. … Yeah fine.

(A moment.)

DEBRA. I'm organising a remembrance.

GINA. I know.

DEBRA. One year.

GINA. I'll help, if I can?

*(**DEBRA** starts to leave.)*

DEBRA. I'll get you bedding.

GINA. Beat me, kick me

> *(**DEBRA** stops.)*

Pull my hair, scream, something…

Something.

> *(**GINA** goes over and embraces her. The moment is awkward for both, but **GINA** holds it.)*

I'm so, so sorry.

> *(**DEBRA** pats her and gently slips out of her hold.)*

DEBRA. Yes.

> *(**DEBRA** leaves. **GINA** looks around the room.)*

3.

What's Been Lost

(Living room – two days later. A series of overlapping news flashes play* – news feeds circle the room. **DEBRA** *gazes at them as she listens on the phone.)*

*(***ALEX***, 23, all passion and energy, sits scanning papers.)*

(Outside – looking in is **LENNY**, *41, solid, a once big presence now slightly shrunken. He watches them until he can't. He hurries away.*

REPORTER 1. The government is looking at measures...

REPORTER 3. Ministers are preparing an action plan...

REPORTER 2. Attempting to find solutions to try and combat teenage violence...

REPORTER 1. Thirty-seven people...

REPORTER 3. Thirty-eight...

REPORTER 1. Thirty-nine have been the victim of teenage violence...

REPORTER 2. The public is asking for tougher penalties...

REPORTER 1. The government wants to implement stricter penalties...

REPORTER 3. Local communities are demanding greater penalties for anyone caught carrying an offensive weapon...

---

* A licence to produce WHAT'S LOST does not include a performance licence for any third-party or copyrighted recordings. Licensees should create their own. Please see note on page iv.

(**ALEX** *watches* **DEBRA** *pace as she gets more wound up by the official on the other end of the phone.*)

DEBRA. I don't see why there's a problem... Then is it not possible to just put extra bins out... No, it didn't occur to me. I'm organising a remembrance for my daughter, rubbish bins didn't seem top priority... That's great they understand, thank them for their understanding, what can they do about it... Right...right... Then... I'll have to, I'll call... tomorrow... I'll call.

(*She cuts the caller off.*)

Tossers.

(*She stays for a moment with her head bowed.* **ALEX** *looks at her, considers. He drops his papers, goes over and very gently puts his hand on the back of her neck.* **DEBRA** *jumps.*)

ALEX. I didn't mean/

DEBRA. No?

ALEX. Anything/

DEBRA. No/

ALEX. I just, you, you looked like

DEBRA. Right

ALEX. Thought you needed

DEBRA. It's how I look

ALEX. Sorry/

DEBRA. Not a come on.

(*A moment.*)

ALEX. It helps, sometimes just... putting a hand on someone, a space. Wherever you see pain... stress. Calms it.

(**DEBRA** *stares at him.*)

Let's have a drink.

(*Silence.*)

Anything I say now'll sound shit, so let's have a drink and forget it

DEBRA. We need to get on.

ALEX. Okay.

(*They both turn away and make a face.* **ALEX** *returns to his papers. After a while of silent shuffling,* **ALEX** *drops them again.*)

What are we doing?

(**DEBRA** *looks at him.*)

Going through and through permits, agreements, why?

DEBRA. Ensuring everything is ready.

ALEX. On paper that's pretty much it.

DEBRA. Checking that unlike the rubbish bin saga, it's actually been done right.

ALEX. Too late if not.

DEBRA. If you have something else to do/

ALEX. I'm not saying that/

DEBRA. go/

ALEX. it's just/

DEBRA. You volunteered yourself.

ALEX. Yeah I want to/

DEBRA. All willing at the beginning, four months in who's left?

ALEX. I'm just/

DEBRA. What?

ALEX. Looking... deeper.

What will this achieve?

>*(She stares at him.)*

DEBRA. Alex/

ALEX. We need to aim for something bigger/

DEBRA. I told everybody when we started, it's not a political campaign.

ALEX. What is it?

DEBRA. A remembrance.

ALEX. Why?

DEBRA. So people remember.

ALEX. That's what you want?

DEBRA. Remembering's generally what you have a remembrance for.

ALEX. I understand/

DEBRA. No you can't. You can't understand. You think your sympathy equals real understanding?

It doesn't.

>*(Silence.)*

I don't want speakers.

ALEX. Yeah, no, I know but/

DEBRA. Politicians, councillors, celebrities, speaking/

ALEX. Draws more people/

DEBRA. Regurgitating sentiments we already know/

ALEX. Gets them to listen/

DEBRA. Who wants to hear?

ALEX. Give them a chance

DEBRA. I work with people who don't listen. Just want me to stick a tick by their name at the end of the day. If they don't want to, nothing will make them not even their presence.

ALEX. Yeah that's business/

DEBRA. We've heard every word that could possibly be spoken and where has it led?

ALEX. So what we, we, we, stop?

DEBRA. I believed in words before…

I'm not going over this. It's not a night for speeches. All I can do is be there for people to see, remember. Her. Him. Us. This is… what's been lost. Not one moment, one day, we're here, one year on and there's no end to it, none. See the consequences, see where one person's action has brought us all.

ALEX. That's great, yeah but/

DEBRA. There are no words, you need to witness, feel. That's what this is.

ALEX. Sitting with candles in a park?

DEBRA. People respond to their gut

ALEX. Yeah/

DEBRA. See a missing person appeal you want to find, bring them back.

(**ALEX** *becomes more worked up.*)

ALEX. Yeah, yeah, yeah, yeah, just being there can stir them yeah, but after, when people go home. We're giving nothing. Nothing for them to take action over. It's an opportunity

DEBRA. For who?

ALEX. For us all to think, to get talking about/

DEBRA. Talking

ALEX. Hostility towards young people. Project closures, truancy and exclusions, living with past perceptions, all the problems young people face.

DEBRA. Right.

ALEX. We can get people thinking about building up relationships in communities, truly addressing mental health, emotional stability and vulnerability.

There's all this stuff we think we know about but not everyone does, cos why's nothing changing? We should be having real conversations about… fear, risk, trauma, stuff that hangs round us

DEBRA. Us?

ALEX. Look where ignoring it's brought everyone. There's nothing more important than this right now, it's part of everything. All these people together… this is a chance to open things up and have real conversations about them/

DEBRA. My responsibility/

ALEX. I'm not saying/

DEBRA. I should give up more of myself?

ALEX. I just think they should take away more than a feeling.

DEBRA. What? Expressive words, excessive emotion? Parents against knives? Or maybe we can get Mr Blair back. He can step up, speak out on the negatives of acting colour blind. We can hire an actor, sportsman and a pop star to give it the sex factor, up the head count. To top it off I can get up to breakdown before them all. They can all go away saying we witnessed that, sad, sad black woman, we understand, before climbing back into their lives to forget. They're not having me. They have her. They took her. They can't have more.

I won't go to breakdown, I don't do breakdowns, sorry I don't.

(Silence.)

She liked candles. She liked silence.

ALEX. Liked debating stuff too

DEBRA. I know, I know. Now it's happened, I've lived this everyone expects something of use, some response some... offer of an answer.

ALEX. I'm not saying that/

DEBRA. Now I should be able to speak about all these things you say. Tell everyone what needs to be done. Well I can't.

(A moment.)

Sorry.

ALEX. No, no/

DEBRA. *(Suddenly.)* I'm just so fucking angry.

And I can't be.

ALEX. Yeah, yeah you can.

DEBRA. No, I can't.

(Silence.)

We'll have a drink.

*(**DEBRA** leaves the room. **ALEX** takes a deep, deep breath, he adjusts himself.)*

*(**DEBRA** returns with a bottle of vodka and glasses. She stops.)*

I want there to be some, meaning. But I don't know what that can be.

If we lived in some ancient time, be easy. Just sacrifice something and believe.

(*Silence.*)

It helps, you coming over, helping.

ALEX. That's good.

DEBRA. I doubt... As time passes, I doubt the worth

ALEX. Don't do that.

DEBRA. I can't help it.

ALEX. What you're doing's excellent, straight.

(**DEBRA** *looks at him for a moment.*)

DEBRA. Why are you?

ALEX. Why?

DEBRA. Involved?

ALEX. ... To help, be active, you know?

DEBRA. I don't know why anybody does anything now.

ALEX. Someone has to do something or, we'll never grow, never go anywhere.

DEBRA. You're so young.

(*A moment.*)

ALEX. Kids on our project. Half of them think nothing of themselves really, ultimately. They're not psychopaths, not most of them. Just, if you think nothing of yourself what will you do for other people? They see gangs have importance, they want in on it. That becomes their family and everyone else is outside. People who wanna take advantage of them get it and use it. It's time the rest of us caught up.

DEBRA. He wasn't in a gang.

ALEX. It's part of the same problem/

DEBRA. Everyone's making it part/

ALEX. Being in one carrying round the weapon of one cos of fear.

DEBRA. She's become one of the statistics and it wasn't even part

ALEX. It's all part

DEBRA. This can't be about him.

ALEX. We're all part. Parents, teachers, park-keepers, waste collectors, anyone on the street. We all have to get involved and take care of each other cos… nothing can change till we get it together and make it.

DEBRA. You're very young.

ALEX. Twenty-three

DEBRA. Do you know what that means?

ALEX. … I'm just me.

(They stare at each other.)

DEBRA. Good having you. Your energy.

ALEX. Let me use it.

(She smiles at him.)

Where's Lenny?

DEBRA. Away.

ALEX. Hasn't come round?

DEBRA. You should get home.

ALEX. We done?

DEBRA. No.

(A moment.)

Was there something… you and… was there anything?

ALEX. We got on.

DEBRA. Yes

ALEX. I liked her, she was, smart

DEBRA. Yes

ALEX. She listened she really understood what was being said. She was bright and just, yeah. Really, really likeable. Only started working with us.

DEBRA. …

ALEX. She stuck with me?

DEBRA. Tragedy does.

ALEX. No, something of her

(**GINA** *comes in. She's been drinking.*)

GINA. Evening,

(*She looks at* **DEBRA**.)

Sorry. Turned out to be an earlier night than I expected. Alright to come in?

DEBRA. Yes. Yes.

(**GINA** *looks* **ALEX** *over.*)

GINA. Hi,

DEBRA. Alex, Gina. My sister.

ALEX. Yeah?

GINA. Hiya Alex.

ALEX. Alright.

DEBRA. Alex is helping, working with me on the remembrance.

GINA. Ah, that's fantastic.

(**GINA** *looks at them both.*)

Not fucking up your meeting am I?

DEBRA. We've finished.

GINA. Excellent, drinks then?

DEBRA. We're just done, Alex is off.

GINA. Have a drink, you can stop for a drink. One.

ALEX. Well, yeah alright.

>   (**GINA** *goes for the bottle.* **DEBRA** *gives her a look.*)

GINA. There anything I can help with?

ALEX. Could do with another opinion on some things

GINA. Ask away.

ALEX. What d'you think about there being a few speakers?

DEBRA. Seriously?

ALEX. Let's hear one more view

DEBRA. It's decided.

>   (**ALEX** *smiles...* **DEBRA** *relents.*)

Well big sister, what would you go for?

>   (**GINA** *looks at* **DEBRA**.)

GINA. You've not really told me much about any of it.

DEBRA. Gina's just arrived.

GINA. Two whole days ago.

DEBRA. We've not had a chance to speak.

GINA. She won't speak to me.

ALEX. Why's that?

GINA. I fucked up big

ALEX. Yeah?

(A moment.)

GINA. I didn't come for… Rudi

ALEX. … How come?

(GINA just stares, she moves away.)

DEBRA. *(To ALEX.)* You should probably go.

ALEX. Sorry if I asked the wrong thing yeah?

GINA. Don't go

DEBRA. It's been a long day/

GINA. It's pissing down out there. Want to end your night with frizz up hair like this?

DEBRA. Thank you Alex.

(A moment.)

ALEX. Yeah alright, we'll speak.

GINA. Sorry

DEBRA. Tomorrow.

ALEX. Yeah.

DEBRA. … If you can.

ALEX. Tomorrow. *(To GINA.)* Good to meet you.

(DEBRA watches him go.)

GINA. Sweet.

DEBRA. Boy.

GINA. Fit one.

DEBRA. Young.

GINA. You wouldn't?

DEBRA. …

GINA. If there was no Lenny I mean?

DEBRA. You shouldn't be thinking it.

GINA. No harm. It's the thing, at the moment.

DEBRA. Little boys?

GINA. He's not that little, and please don't joke about that.

DEBRA. You're the one thinking it.

GINA. Old enough, young enough.

> *(An old routine, but* **DEBRA** *doesn't want to play.)*

DEBRA. I'm off, need some sleep.

GINA. It's early.

DEBRA. I need an early night.

GINA. Used to do anything to stay awake with me. No matter how closed your eyes got or how many times your head dropped. Or how many times mum came to the door long after they tucked us in. You used to compete with me to stay up.

DEBRA. …

GINA. Copied me in everything.

DEBRA. Not everything

GINA. Wet looked your hair just after I did

DEBRA. Everyone had a wet look then

GINA. Pressed it straight after I did too

DEBRA. It's called fashion, you didn't invent it.

GINA. You could've taken the cane row route

DEBRA. I wasn't into it

GINA. Yeah cos I wasn't.

DEBRA. Believe what you like.

GINA. Begged mum to make you the same pinafore dresses as me too.

DEBRA. When I was ten.

GINA. Pretend your ten now

>   (**DEBRA** *gives her a look.*)

Come on, have a likkle drink with me.

DEBRA. Ten year olds don't drink

GINA. We'd get a little sip on a Sunday

DEBRA. ...

GINA. ...

DEBRA. No.

GINA. Talk to me then, two days and you've hardly said anything. Talk to me. A talk, just talk. *(Intensely.)* Come on Dee give something, give me/

DEBRA. What?

GINA. ... Sorry

>   *(Silence.)*

I went over to Nadine's. Sends you love.

DEBRA. How is she?

GINA. Stopped drinking.

My old drinking mate's stopped drinking.

>   *(She laughs a bit.)*

Patronising, she was... as patronising as you can be, being a single mum living in a studio come bedsit in zone four.

DEBRA. Not a good night

GINA. Kept stuffing herself with baby food, what's that about?

DEBRA. Child not feeding.

GINA. Don't recognise her anymore.

DEBRA. She's grown, moved on.

GINA. Grown ugly

DEBRA. You leave people behind

GINA. And fat

DEBRA. Once they stop being like you.

GINA. Smug and bloated

DEBRA. Maybe it's time/

GINA. Shit night, and I end it with shit hair on top.

DEBRA. Go to bed.

GINA. Can't sleep. Can't work. Nothing, nothing comes out at the moment.

DEBRA. Well…

GINA. Can't connect this brain to physical action.

DEBRA. Really

GINA. Can't.

Met this guy. Put my concentration out.

Never used to be so susceptible.

Once it was all art.

DEBRA. Can't live on art.

(Silence.)

GINA. Please have one drink with me. Let's drink, talk

*(**DEBRA** relents. She pours herself the tiniest glass and raises it to **GINA**.)*

Meant a proper measure not mouthwash

> (**DEBRA** *gives her a look, a smile, between them.*)

DEBRA. Who was the, guy?

> (**GINA** *smiles at her.*)

GINA. Dejan. Serbian. Thought he was Russian, sounded Russian, well how you imagine Russian sounds.

Spoke from his gut, straight.

Beautiful. Beautiful face, fantastically sculpt-able. Dark, with starved features, you know that kind of gaunt?

DEBRA. Not your typical Russian then.

GINA. No he's Serbian.

DEBRA. … Didn't work out?

GINA. What's up with me?

DEBRA. Too late for therapy.

GINA. Everything slips

DEBRA. Get some rest.

GINA. Keep… losing things.

Drawing, even drawing even… loved sketching over and over, hope of getting it there, getting it down right. Even that's slipping away, my belief

DEBRA. Belief

> (*There is a moment of recognition between them.*)

GINA. Love you.

DEBRA. I need sleep.

GINA. No time to chat about Russian looking Serbs.

DEBRA. I have a lot on.

GINA. I know... I know. And it's great this. A remembrance, great you're getting it together doing something. It's big.

DEBRA. We'll see.

GINA. I'll help, just ask. Yeah? Just call on me.

DEBRA. Night.

GINA. Night night then.

*(**GINA** watches her go.)*

Sweet dreams. I wish you, sweet ones.

*(**GINA** looks round the room. She downs half the bottle of vodka.)*

4.

Thought You Were Such a Different Person

>*(Living room.* **LENNY** *stands looking down at* **GINA**. *She's collapsed on the settee with a throw covering her.)*

LENNY. Heavy night?

GINA. Who's that?

LENNY. Who d'you reckon?

GINA. … Lenny.

LENNY. Afternoon.

GINA. What?

LENNY. One-thirty.

GINA. Fuck.

>*(She looks at the throw covering her.)*

LENNY. You alright?

GINA. … Yeah. Yeah, you know.

>*(She smiles at him.)*

Dee said you'd gone away.

LENNY. Just, living low.

>*(**LENNY** bends and kisses her on the cheek. He straightens up immediately.)*

Breath.

GINA. Just alcohol,

LENNY. Smell it from here.

GINA. Only vodka.

LENNY. Yeah and some.

GINA. ... Living low?

> (**LENNY** *walks looking around as he talks.*)

LENNY. Needed time away.

GINA. Know that one.

> (*He stops to look at her for a moment.*)

LENNY. Great you came.

> (*She looks at him.*)

Meant that genuinely.

GINA. I know, know you... Sorry, before. I couldn't.

LENNY. Yeah/

GINA. Stupid decision.

LENNY. Yeah, but its done

GINA. Most stupid I've ever been.

Won't be forgiven,

LENNY. I forgive you.

> (*She stares at him.*)

GINA. Do you?

LENNY. Why hold on to it?

GINA. ... Thanks.

LENNY. Wish I hadn't...

> (*A moment.*)

You're looking... reasonable.

GINA. Fuck off.

LENNY. Hardly say fantastic when you've just got up.

(They smile warmly at each other.)

GINA. Well?

LENNY. What?

GINA. Make us a coffee.

LENNY. Give us a chance.

GINA. I'm the guest here mate.

LENNY. You're family

GINA. A family guest, get in that kitchen and get the kettle boiling.

(GINA rubs her face. LENNY just stays watching.)

One thirty. Dee gone to work?

LENNY. Course.

GINA. She hasn't stopped moving.

(LENNY stays quiet.)

GINA. How is it?

LENNY. What d'you think?

GINA. …

LENNY. It's quiet, very quiet.

(Silence.)

GINA. I couldn't take it. That's why… couldn't come back, couldn't pretend not to see

(There is a moment as GINA realises the honesty of this.)

Rudi was like me, part of me… I just couldn't

LENNY. You know she'd sit me in her room and make me listen to her music. Listened to the latest track she was into.

Only did it to laugh at how I took it. But I'd surprise her, whatever she put on I liked. I was so proud of her taste. Her music's gone.

GINA. Staying away was so stupid.

>   *(**LENNY** just looks at her.)*

I can feel Dee raging at me for it. And now's not time.

LENNY. Well time's fucked at the moment.

GINA. ... You look good.

LENNY. Yeah?

GINA. What's this? Texting me to come and not being around?

LENNY. How d'you want your coffee?

GINA. ... Black, three sugars.

>   *(**LENNY** goes to make coffee.)*

Cheers.

>   *(**GINA** sits for a second then jumps up. She rolls up the throw. Picks at her hair, checks her reflection in the vodka bottle, gives up.)*

*(Shouting to **LENNY**.)* Toast'd be good.

>   *(She places the bottle in a corner. She stops to stare at it. She looks around. She finds a candle and forces it to fit into the top of the bottle. She places it somewhere prominent. **LENNY** re-enters with coffee. He glances at the candle.)*

LENNY. You sleeping in here?

GINA. Collapsed in here. Can't you tell by the unwrapped hair?

(LENNY grins at her.)

Yeah alright.

(She picks at it again.)

Toast?

LENNY. No bread.

GINA. She always has bread in.

LENNY. Two of you talk?

GINA. Not done real conversation since we were eight?

LENNY. You're just opposites.

GINA. That's a kind description.

(She smiles. He smiles.)

LENNY. How's work, that… rapping… trainers idea you were working on? Anything happening?

GINA. It's on hold.

LENNY. Yeah?

GINA. Apparently four to seven year olds would be confused by the concept.

LENNY. Shame

GINA. Can't have an inanimate object rapping about promoting peace.

LENNY. Why not make it a human?

GINA. … Because it's not.

LENNY. Right.

GINA. It's not just another cartoon,

LENNY. I thought it was?

GINA. It's an intelligent animation film for young people,

LENNY. Okay

GINA. It's for them to use their imagination, to think about things from an alien point of view.

LENNY. Yeah right, I get you. I get it.

GINA. No one gets it that's the problem. Sometimes think I'm on this solo wavelength no one can tune in on.

Rudi got it.

> (**LENNY** *gazes at her.*)

Anyway. It's there, ready for whenever everyone else catches up. I'll get back to it sometime. See the difference in another year, Shove it in again when tastes change, or producers do.

> (**LENNY** *very suddenly touches her face. He holds it, moves up very close to her.* **GINA**'s *stunned for a second before moving back. He shakes his head and quickly moves away.*)

LENNY. Sorry

GINA. What was that?

> (**LENNY** *is silent.*)

Lenny?

> (*He turns away from her.*)

Lenny?

LENNY. We've split.

We've split up.

GINA. What?

LENNY. Dee an me. We split.

GINA. ... When?

(He shakes his head.)

LENNY. Just couldn't

GINA. And that was what?

LENNY. Just needed to/

GINA. Fuck Lenny, fuck…

It's not a time to separate.

LENNY. There isn't a time.

GINA. You both need support, it's not a time to disappear.

(She waits. He stays silent.)

Why?

LENNY. I wanna forget.

GINA. You should…

I don't know… what do I know.

LENNY. …

GINA. …

LENNY. She's loaded up. Running about, all the time.

Constant work, this… remembrance. New obsession. Running about with her little helper. What's it for?

We don't need reminding.

GINA. Splitting's… wrong.

*(**LENNY** stays quiet.)*

GINA. Why didn't you say?

LENNY. Would you have come?

GINA. She's hard, I know/

LENNY. You didn't come to the funeral.

GINA. Told you/

LENNY. Would you ever have come back if I hadn't texted you?

GINA. ...

LENNY. She needs help/

GINA. Won't want me.

LENNY. Just be here, for a bit

GINA. She won't take anything from me.

LENNY. I tried.

GINA. Tried

LENNY. Yeah

GINA. ...

LENNY. ...

GINA. Such a weak word, weak action. Tried.

I fail trying all the time. Shouldn't try.

Do. Do it.

LENNY. Do it? What am I? We're not... people aren't granite.

You think you just do? Continue and do, whatever the sadness, the hardness of it?

GINA. *(Gently.)* Alright.

LENNY. There's no way to be. That's how it is, there isn't a normal. It's gone, been taken and there's no way of being after that.

(Silence.)

GINA. Where are you?

LENNY. Here... and away, mainly away.

GINA. Where?

LENNY. A mate's.

GINA. Mate?

LENNY. … Sereena's.

GINA. Right.

LENNY. She's got her little helper but I'm the cunt.

GINA. Yeah.

LENNY. The weak one.

GINA. Right.

LENNY. Nothing you do can be right. That's how it is Gina. That's what it is for us now.

GINA. I can't be here on my own.

LENNY. She needs someone.

GINA. I can't/

LENNY. She's your sister.

>   (**GINA** *glares at him.*)

GINA. Thought you were such a different person.

LENNY. …

GINA. …

LENNY. I tried.

GINA. … Right.

5.

Something Must Happen

(Overlapping news flashes and news feeds.*
Inside, living room – **GINA** *checks her mobile for messages.)*

(Outside – **DEBRA** *and* **LENNY** *stand staring at each other.)*

REPORTER 1. A fourteen year old boy has been stabbed...

REPORTER 2. Was left bleeding in the street...

REPORTER 3. Stabbed earlier this afternoon...

REPORTER 2. Stabbed just hours ago near Croydon high street...

REPORTER 1. Police say it is unclear...

REPORTER 3. Local residents say it is clear...

REPORTER 1. The government say they can't be clear...

REPORTER 2. A local man has described the lack of attention that was given to a number of previous incidents...

LENNY. Hey

*(***DEBRA** *nods.)*

(Neither knows what to say for a long time, till **DEBRA** *breaks it.)*

DEBRA. Haven't been alone since I was twenty. Not physically.

---

* A licence to produce WHAT'S LOST does not include a performance licence for any third-party or copyrighted recordings. Licensees should create their own. Please see note on page iv.

LENNY. You don't have to be.

> (**DEBRA** *stays quiet.*)

> (**LENNY** *moves up close to her.*)

LENNY. Look at you

> (*A moment.*)

Wanna suck you in, feel you.

> (*He touches her.*)

Be inside... deep

DEBRA. Deep

LENNY. Deep in you. I want that.

DEBRA. Appropriate.

LENNY. Still.

DEBRA. ...still

LENNY. More.

DEBRA. Yes.

LENNY. Fuck appropriate.

DEBRA. Easy for you.

LENNY. How?

DEBRA. Lenny

LENNY. Why d'you think things are easier for me?

DEBRA. ...

LENNY. How is it?

> (*A moment.*)

DEBRA. Can't just

LENNY. What?

(**DEBRA** *shakes her head.*)

Speak to me.

DEBRA. Then you'd have to speak back.

LENNY. ...

DEBRA. Still nothing

LENNY. Give me a chance.

DEBRA. There's not time for chances.

LENNY. You kill me every time.

DEBRA. ... I don't mean to.

LENNY. ...

DEBRA. ...

LENNY. Make you close to her doing this?

DEBRA. I'm doing what I can

LENNY. Should be us together, not a load of strangers, there.

(**DEBRA** *stays quiet.*)

LENNY. Don't have this thing. It's too soon for us.

DEBRA. Us?

LENNY. Being in a park with a load of kids making it something else.

How's that gonna help you and me?

(*She moves away.*)

Do it next year, the one after if you have to.

DEBRA. It's planned.

LENNY. Doesn't matter, doesn't mean anything. Not what anyone's done, what they're gonna do. If you wanna step away you can.

DEBRA. Something must happen.

> (**LENNY** *just stares at her.*)

You're a giant. Married you because you were such a giant.

LENNY. Married you to watch you come every night.

> (*An old joke.* **DEBRA** *smiles briefly.*)

DEBRA. Yes.

LENNY. We could go off somewhere, make time.

Tell them you need time, if you need to explain anything to anybody.

DEBRA. I can't

LENNY. So you just go ahead no matter what that means to me?

> (**DEBRA** *turns away. He looks at her for the longest time. Then reality hits him.*)

This it? Is it?

DEBRA. Lenny

LENNY. Don't want it to be

DEBRA. …

LENNY. She wouldn't want it.

DEBRA. …

LENNY. Is it?

> (**LENNY** *waits, there's nothing from* **DEBRA**.)

> (*He backs down.*)

> (*He walks away.*)

6.

Something Must

> (**RUDI**'s *room. As news flashes/feeds pass around her**. **DEBRA** *stands in the dark of* **RUDI**'s *room asking herself over and over.*)

DEBRA. How do I... how do I respond.

REPORTER 3. Community workers say it's essential to look at different approaches following the latest incident...

REPORTER 1. Local people are demanding a rise in the number of stop and searches...

> (**DEBRA** *moves trapped around the room.*)

REPORTER 3. The black community is wary of the consequences of targeted stop and searches...

REPORTER 2. Ministers are asking that paperwork be reduced to free officers...

REPORTER 1. The Mayor's office has set up a new unit to deal with rising street violence in the capital...

> (*A news flash/feed of a politician speaking about the importance of safety and how stop and search is key to it...**)

> (**DEBRA** *tries to breath in* **RUDI**, *tries to hold onto something. She sees* **RUDI**.)

---

* A licence to produce WHAT'S LOST does not include a performance licence for any third-party or copyrighted recordings. Licensees should create their own. Please see note on page iv.

7.

Stand Up

(Living room. **GINA** *sits gazing at her mobile, willing a call, something.* **DEBRA** *watches her for a moment before coming in.)*

GINA. Hey. Thought you were working?

DEBRA. Seen the news?

GINA. Never put the TV on before seven.

DEBRA. Right.

GINA. …

DEBRA. Here all morning?

GINA. Drank a bit much last night. Thanks for the cover.

*(***DEBRA** *dosen't respond.)*

GINA. What is it, what's up?

DEBRA. The world

GINA. Yeah, big one

DEBRA. There was a stabbing.

GINA. Another?

*(***DEBRA** *dosen't respond.)*

GINA. Well… well

DEBRA. Yes.

(Silence.)

GINA. Get you a drink? Coffee?

DEBRA. No

GINA. Stronger?

DEBRA. Why not.

(**GINA** *gets her a drink.* **DEBRA** *notices the vodka bottle with candle.*)

GINA. Wine alright?

(**DEBRA** *takes it and drinks.*)

DEBRA. It's so quiet.

GINA. Except for traffic.

DEBRA. Barely hear it.

GINA. And the builders over the road.

DEBRA. Always something being built.

Never enough buildings, shame they don't fill them.

(*They stand in silence for a moment.*)

GINA. Wanted to ask. Could you spare... something?

DEBRA. ...

GINA. Had a problem with... getting anything out.

(**DEBRA** *stares.*)

Don't worry if you can't. I'll go to the bank, sort whatever it is, I just thought maybe, meantime, you could, but if you don't have it I'm okay

DEBRA. I'm not thinking about money

GINA. Well what is it?

DEBRA. Nothing Gina.

GINA. No it is something,

DEBRA. It's nothing

GINA. Just say.

DEBRA. Yes.

GINA. There wasn't a question in that.

DEBRA. My mind's busy.

>   *(A moment.)*

GINA. … I could do some work?

DEBRA. What?

GINA. Work for you, or one of your… colleagues if it's easier. Answer calls, whatever needs doing. Help out.

DEBRA. Not really/

GINA. There must be something.

DEBRA. Gina

GINA. Yeah?

>   *(**GINA** waits, **DEBRA** doesn't say more.)*

Lenny was in.

DEBRA. Right. Are you staying around or travelling?

GINA. … Not made up my mind.

DEBRA. Well you should. You need to do something.

Start getting things together. You've got your life you really shouldn't waste it.

GINA. Been here less than a week.

DEBRA. And asking to be paid for it.

GINA. Don't

DEBRA. Aren't you?

>   *(A moment.)*

GINA. I'm only asking about help you offered.

DEBRA. Right.

GINA. Things, financially, aren't great for me at the moment.

DEBRA. Work

GINA. I'm trying, that's what I'm asking you for, so I can, breathe, get on.

DEBRA. Why don't you teach?

GINA. … I'm not a teacher.

DEBRA. But you could do it.

GINA. It's not what I am.

DEBRA. You can't just be what you like.

GINA. Not arguing. There's bigger things, why do we… have to always argue?

(**GINA** *stares at her, she looks away.*)

It's hard… hard. Can't just do any job. Get into the money and I lose, that becomes what I am and I can't do that now, not… after all this time.

Even if I want to, even if I seem to have become a caricature of myself to you. I can't give up now.

DEBRA. Mum and dad left/

GINA. Twenty grand Dee not twenty million

DEBRA. Have some respect

GINA. I do

DEBRA. They worked fucking hard/

GINA. I know, I respect everything they did

DEBRA. Just couldn't be there.

(**GINA** *looks down.*)

GINA. I respect everything. Left all they could, not disrespecting... just saying it wasn't an ever lasting fund.

DEBRA. Christ

GINA. It's not meant badly

DEBRA. Nothing means anything with you.

GINA. What's that mean?

DEBRA. I can't be responsible for how you choose to live.

GINA. I didn't ask you to/

DEBRA. I'm busy. I'm busy, do you understand? My mind is busy, busy, it's busy, I'm busy.

*(**GINA** goes out. She comes back.)*

GINA. ...

DEBRA. ...

GINA. Lenny said you've split

DEBRA. Yes.

GINA. Why didn't you say?

DEBRA. When?

GINA. What?

DEBRA. ... There was no chance.

GINA. Last night?

DEBRA. When you wanted to talk?

GINA. When I wanted you to talk to me

DEBRA. You came back to talk about your life. That's what we do Gina. Talk about how things are for you. Now mum and dad have gone, I listen, I comment, I slip you spare change.

(**GINA** *goes out. She comes straight back jacket in hand.*)

GINA. Why do you have to do this/

DEBRA. Your life isn't working.

GINA. So what, I should, what should I?

DEBRA. Do something different.

GINA. You don't get it

DEBRA. How long are you going to keep on?

GINA. What, should I …attempt suicide?

DEBRA. You live like you just left art college.

GINA. What's wrong with living in hope?

DEBRA. You're over forty

GINA. So?

DEBRA. It's time to stop relying on it.

GINA. I did. I did. I went for something concrete.

Bought my concrete fucking council flat, just like you… you pushed me to do and… it's gone.

DEBRA. What?

GINA. They've taken it

DEBRA. …

GINA. See. Concrete doesn't exist.

DEBRA. You lost the flat?

GINA. It slipped away like everything else.

DEBRA. And you're here.

GINA. Stop pushing/

DEBRA. That's why/

GINA. You've got to stop/

DEBRA. You've nowhere else/

GINA. It's not to do with/

DEBRA. /Can't believe you/

GINA. /Didn't come cos of that/

DEBRA. /I can't believe you let it go/

GINA. /You're my sister/

DEBRA. /because you won't be responsible/

GINA. /What're you talking about/

DEBRA. Things won't magically be all right because you live in a cloud called hope, you have to work for it/

GINA. You're supposed to be there for me/

DEBRA. I won't fund you're lifestyle

GINA. I wasn't asking/

DEBRA. Fund you and your "cartoon creativity"/

GINA. Yeah I get you hate it/

DEBRA. What right do you have to do nothing/

GINA. I work, I'm an artist

DEBRA. What does it pay for?

GINA. It's shit, it's hard but it's what I can do

DEBRA. It's not a career.

GINA. Don't look down on me.

    (**DEBRA** *goes for her.*)

DEBRA. Then stand up.

    (*A moment.*)

  Stand up, and do something of worth.

    (**GINA** *puts her hands up in surrender.*)

GINA. I can't argue with you anymore

DEBRA. Yes, listen instead of opening your mouth to answer with your rubbish

GINA. ... I chose, different,

DEBRA. Right.

GINA. And this, this isn't my fault

DEBRA. Yes, right

GINA. Don't look down on me for my choice

DEBRA. Scummy little artist with nothing.

> (**GINA** *pulls a handful of change from her pocket and chucks it at her sister.* **DEBRA** *grabs her, lifts her off the ground. She stops, drops* **GINA**, *kicks out at the bottle and candle it falls, smashes.*)

You squander... everything, everything, life, talent, people's... feelings... people, mum, dad, you just walk off

GINA. You always judge/

DEBRA. Rudi/

GINA. I loved her/

DEBRA. You have no responsibility/

GINA. I loved Rudi

DEBRA. Did you listen, did you ever listen, or just encourage her to leave herself all open an free, an immune to reality like you?

GINA. ...

DEBRA. You, you pushed her into the same cloud you live in.

GINA. You can't blame me

DEBRA. And when the worst, the worst happens you couldn't even turn up, couldn't respect, you have no care, no... involvement, nothing, nothing is real for you, hop in and fuck off again.

What's that? What is that?

> (**GINA** *rushes out.*)
>
> (**DEBRA** *hits, hits, hits out. She sees* **RUDI**. *She moves away,* **RUDI** *follows, tries to hold her.* **DEBRA** *yells...*)
>
> (**DEBRA** *alone. She stares at the smashed glass. She gathers herself back together and very slowly, very controlled picks up the pieces.*)

8.

People Shouldn't Be Able To Walk Into You

(Living room. **DEBRA** *is alone. Headlines from news feeds* circle the room. The doorbell rings. She ignores it. It rings again, and again. There is silence then her mobile goes. She looks at the number, chucks it down still ringing. She goes to answer the door.)*

(She comes back with **ALEX**.*)*

ALEX. If you didn't want to talk, you only had to answer and say.

DEBRA. And you would have disappeared?

ALEX. …

DEBRA. Heard the news?

ALEX. Yeah.

DEBRA. And you've some suggestion? Some argument? Some… something we should do.

ALEX. Came to check you were okay.

DEBRA. Right.

*(**ALEX** sees the money scattered on the floor, he starts to pick it up.)*

Leave it.

(He looks at her, leaves it.)

I was thinking.

---

* A licence to produce WHAT'S LOST does not include a performance licence for any third-party or copyrighted recordings. Licensees should create their own. Please see note on page iv.

ALEX. Tell me.

DEBRA. Maybe we deserve to die... We deserve to go nowhere, to achieve nothing. Because we don't learn. We don't have the confidence to learn and do better.

ALEX. Should I go?

DEBRA. No I want you to hear.

ALEX. I hear.

DEBRA. He should have been properly punished.

Punished properly.

ALEX. ...

DEBRA. People shouldn't be able to walk into you and, smash you, crush everything and... just walk on.

ALEX. ...

DEBRA. They need to bring back the death penalty.

They should. They need too.

ALEX. Listen/

DEBRA. I listen, I hear your compassion, your... humanity, but I think crime should be punished.

ALEX. It's understandable/

DEBRA. Throats should be cut, insides removed and passed on to decent human beings that will use them properly. There should be electrocutions, decapitations, burning, real bloody, scummy punishments.

Stick criminals in a ring, till they rip each other up like the scum they are, treat them like the stupid scum they aspire to be.

ALEX. You're just upset/

DEBRA. Sorry I can't be nice anymore

(She turns on him.)

And I blame, I do anyone... thick enough to suggest we throw love and understanding at it.

Give respect to those who give none?

What's that?

ALEX. You're angry/

DEBRA. I'm allowed.

ALEX. I think you should/

DEBRA. Sorry it's not nice. I can't be nice.

I can't.

(Silence.)

What do you think?

ALEX. What?

DEBRA. Really? What do you feel, what's there, inside?

ALEX. I ... I'm just me, yeah.

DEBRA. Go on.

ALEX. Can't get into this.

DEBRA. Don't hide now. Give me something.

ALEX. You can't hear.

DEBRA. I'm waiting

*(**ALEX** begins to shake.)*

ALEX. If they built a youth club tomorrow and filled it with love, respect the latest iPhone and PS whatever I don't know if any of it would be different.

DEBRA. Good.

ALEX. But I hope.

DEBRA. ... Hope.

ALEX. Yeah. And do what I can.

DEBRA. Hope.

ALEX. Cos if the alternative's... what you suggest.

Just to punish, to have harder and harder punishments

DEBRA. Yes.

ALEX. We're doing nothing but going backwards.

DEBRA. Maybe backwards is the way forward.

ALEX. ... That thinking will do nothing.

DEBRA. Convince me, convince me, stop these news reports rapping, raging in my head. Just... convince... convince me.

*(**ALEX** is shaking harder now.)*

ALEX. I can only tell you what I see. Things will only work if we can be more... for each other. If we listen, try an respect.

Most of the kids I'm around, they just want opportunities. Someone else created the world they have to get on in yeah, and it's not that fair. The past has divided us.

But if we let that be it, what's the point in people. Everything's possible. But we have to try getting to a place where everyone can be better not worse. What you're saying... that would only make us all worst.

(Long silence.)

*(**DEBRA** looks at him. She holds his arms, strokes them to stop him shaking. He moves away. She moves with him. She looks into his face for the longest time.)*

DEBRA. You arrange it. Arrange what you can.

*(**ALEX** stares at her unsure, she slowly becomes more animated.)*

Ask whoever you want.

Whoever you can get in the time.

ALEX. What you saying?

DEBRA. Arrange what you think will help.

ALEX. You're serious?

DEBRA. We'll see

ALEX. Why've you changed?

DEBRA. You... You are so young

ALEX. ...

DEBRA. Doesn't matter.

ALEX. It's the right thing

DEBRA. People want to make their statements.

ALEX. People want to help.

DEBRA. Yes.

ALEX. Let them.

(A moment.)

DEBRA. Get your project down. Get them to get their friends there. I'll go up. I'll stand up, say something.

*(**ALEX** smiles, plans running through his mind.)*

ALEX. Attract them with whoever we can get, whoever they look to... those that could be out with something tomorrow. Get as many people as we can down. I'll get some of the guys at the project to speak. Have people around that can see them, that can listen. Get them to hear, to, to, to, to see everyone affected, maybe it can... maybe.

DEBRA. Do what we can.

ALEX. All we can, yeah. We'll make this massive.

I'll get on it, get everyone at the project calling on who they know.

DEBRA. Yes.

ALEX. The more people gathered, the more involvement, the more chance it'll reach others.

DEBRA. Then let's reach all we can

> (**ALEX** *stops, reassures.*)

ALEX. It's the crime… that's pointless. Not doing what you can to stop it, to help. It isn't real, punishment.

> *(She looks at him.)*

Nothing's real to them. Not till it happens.

> *(It comes to her. She decides what she's going to do. She moves away from him.)*

DEBRA. … Yes.

9.

Time's Running

(**RUDI**'s *room.* **GINA** *packs the few things she has scattered around into her rucksack and smokes.*)

GINA. Sorry hon... sorry. I was on my way, I was. Couldn't stand coming, but I did. Hitched down. This guy he picked me up. Dejan. I'd been there over an hour hoping this was the last time I ever had to stand on the kerb begging for a ride. Know I always bragged. Freedom of getting around for nothing but no one hitches anymore not even students. World's got scarier. But, you know how things get. Have to think about what I spend every pound on and National Rail won't ever be a consideration. So I'm in a car with... lovely Dejan. I know he's alright, right away. He asks where I want to go and drives in silence, like it's a job. Like... He has to be pressed to speak. I tell him I'm on my way to... to Dee's. I say Dee. Can't say the words that make what's happened definite. So, I say my sister's and stop talking

(**GINA** *takes a long drag.*)

Sit gazing through the window. See a piece of nothing land, straw grass, everything looks like it lives in shadow. Still there's a couple of houses out there, middle of nowhere. Maybe I could... I could build my own home. Get a flatpack. Nowhere land's better than living out of storage again. Catch my reflection... and my face is wet, never felt the tears falling. Start rambling on, about me and Dee growing up. Going to college, ducking all the tags, avoiding the "Leave school as soon as", do admin at the local funeral parlour, get married and move up to Ilford. Can't even afford that now even if I wanted it. Talk about me choosing art. Dee choosing stability.

I'm ranting it all at him, me and Dee turning it on each other, cos there's still differences within difference, and she hates me. *(Pause.)*

I'm rambling about our run ins, our fights. Think he thinks I'm annoying, because, I know I can be really irritating. But when I run dry, he talks like he's listened. Says it's pointless. Just like that, blunt.

"Arguments, divides, battles, hate they are pointless." And he... put his hand on my hand and it's so, warm. *(She takes a long drag.)* We spent the night, your night... together. The next and the next and... I'm sorry things happen at the wrong moment and I have to grab something. Times... running, have to leave something

    (GINA places the rolled canvas on the bed.)

His home, his country he reckons could have been great. Could have won a World Cup, joined together. But now it's split into a load of little places, all because some people want to separate themselves.

Make themselves seem better and they will never be better enough. Makes me smile. I tell him it will be beautiful again. *(She smiles.)* Everything good is revived, eventually.

    (DEBRA comes in, she watches her sister take a last look around the room.)

    (GINA picks up her rucksack. She turns, sees DEBRA.)

DEBRA. What are you doing?

GINA. Just getting myself ready to hit that road.

    (DEBRA stares. GINA carries on, checks the room for anything left.)

DEBRA. You should stay... a few more nights.

GINA. …

DEBRA. If you want to.

GINA. Course I do

DEBRA. For the remembrance.

GINA. Yeah, I really wanna be here for that.

DEBRA. Good

GINA. And if I can help

DEBRA. It's under control.

(Silence.)

GINA. I care, my niece, that's a bond it's own and I do care, I miss… I was just so upset Dee. I'm sorry

I am really

(A moment.)

DEBRA. I have to get on.

GINA. Okay

DEBRA. Fine in the room?

GINA. Fine, yes.

DEBRA. Right.

GINA. Thank you

DEBRA. Good.

GINA. Oh Dee

DEBRA. See you later.

*(**DEBRA** walks away.)*

10.

Chasing Oblivion

(Living room. **DEBRA** *holds two bottles of wine. She tops up* **ALEX** *glass then her own.* **GINA** *and* **ALEX** *watch.)*

GINA. I need to stop drinking.

DEBRA. Why?

GINA. Doesn't work.

DEBRA. You're obviously not getting enough.

*(***DEBRA** *pours wine in* **GINA***'s glass till it is near to spilling.* **GINA** *looks at her then at* **ALEX**.*)*

GINA. It'll be great.

ALEX. Yeah.

GINA. A great tribute.

ALEX. Dizzee's a definite

GINA. Fantastic.

ALEX. Got a mention on London news tonight, should get word round.

GINA. Let me know what I can do. If there's anything. *(To* **DEBRA**.*)* Got your speech?

DEBRA. I'm putting something together.

GINA. I can stand with you?

DEBRA. It's fine.

ALEX. Let's see.

DEBRA. What?

ALEX. Your speech, give it to us.

DEBRA. I'm still thinking.

ALEX. What you've got.

GINA. Come on Dee, make it easier for you.

ALEX. We can maybe give you more ideas.

GINA. Be harder there.

ALEX. Do it once and it'll feel like nothing tomorrow.

DEBRA. I haven't written a speech yet.

(A moment.)

ALEX. Nothing at all?

DEBRA. I have a picture in my head, it will come.

GINA. We could do it together now.

DEBRA. I really don't want to. Let's have more drink.

ALEX. You wanna be fit.

*(**DEBRA** tops up all their glasses.)*

DEBRA. Aids concentration. Getting drunk the night before.

GINA. I always said that.

*(**GINA** watches as **DEBRA** tops herself up again, and downs the glass.)*

DEBRA. Yes.

GINA. You never listened.

DEBRA. Doing things differently.

*(**DEBRA** tops up her glass.)*

GINA. Shouldn't we be doing this after?

DEBRA. It's not a celebration.

(A moment.)

Talk. Talk, take my mind away.

(There's an awkward silence. **GINA** *stares at* **ALEX**.*)*

GINA. *(To* **ALEX**.*)* How old are you?

ALEX. Why?

DEBRA. Old enough, young enough.

GINA. Nineteen?

ALEX. Twenty three.

GINA. Fuck

ALEX. What?

GINA. Twenty three?

ALEX. The number?

DEBRA. The youth.

GINA. I miss twenty three.

DEBRA. You remember it?

GINA. Not details, but I miss it.

ALEX. It's not all that.

GINA. Just starting to do things.

DEBRA. I was getting ready to be a mum.

(A moment.)

GINA. Thirty one was the best. Starting to club again. Old school nights I missed the first time. Being out to four and shagging in corners or at bus stops. Well, still occasionally do that, but the other bits.

Late night chips and kebabs and burgers are definitely tastier after thirty. What do you taste as a kid?

You don't really have taste buds before twenty five.

DEBRA. That doesn't make sense/

GINA. And hangovers. I miss proper hangovers. The heavy kind, not the lightweight ones I get now cos I can't do it anymore.

DEBRA. It's not all about getting drunk. You can relax in a decent bar restaurant, a brasserie. Have fun at a dinner party.

GINA. Suffocate me now and bury me please if all I've got left is that, I hate dinner parties

DEBRA. Depends on the company.

GINA. I hate the conversations and the looks and posh fucking red wine that tastes like TCP with food colouring. You have to look down on the same TV shows, dress in "officially" appropriated designer and laugh at the same people who aren't you.

ALEX. I quite like dinner do's

GINA. You don't go to dinner parties at twenty three

ALEX. ... Yeah I do

DEBRA. They're in.

GINA. And how did desert become a drug substitute? Now everyone just gets fat instead of... orgasmic.

DEBRA. Orgasmic, ancient word.

GINA. And music's just there to underscore the evening instead of being the soul of the night. What's there to like?

ALEX. It's good... going out for conversation getting deep into it.

GINA. Instead of chasing oblivion?

ALEX. Get some serious discussions going.

GINA. That's a meeting not a party.

ALEX. Why?

GINA. Party's not in it so shouldn't use the word. Late night supper meeting. Food, limited alcohol, significant unlimited argument and ditch the mellow background sounds from another decade. There.

Easily distinguishable so you know to avoid it.

ALEX. Well I prefer talking to people. Like it more than getting sweaty and drunk in a dark room.

GINA. Don't let anyone else hear you say that.

ALEX. It's good to discuss, to have opinions and to, to, to want to do something with them.

DEBRA. He's right.

ALEX. Half the shit about is there cos no-one talks. We need to give more. People... people need to take more care of each other.

(*A moment.*)

GINA. You're quite spectacular. Bordering dodgy

DEBRA. Leave him.

ALEX. Dodgy?

GINA. Too much. But you might make a sensational man.

ALEX. I am a man

DEBRA. Intelligent, passionate, compassionate one.

GINA. I'd shag him

DEBRA. Would he have you?

ALEX. ...

GINA. Ah

DEBRA. More drink.

(**GINA** *tops up the glasses.*)

GINA. Need to turn this music up.

> (**GINA** *turns up a track in the style of Nina Simone, or similar.** *They all listen for a moment.*)

Shall we dance?

DEBRA. No

GINA. Please. One thing we always did well together.

DEBRA. Did we?

GINA. The parties, remember them? Mum and Dad's? Our last dance, two of us then up to bed, listening out. Waking up to the last sounds early Sunday morning. Wondering if there was any patties or chow mein left over. Remember that, every party had patties, curry goat and chow mein.

Felt so comforting

> (**GINA** *moves up close to* **DEBRA**.)

Please, dance with me.

> (**GINA** *takes* **DEBRA**'s *hand and pulls her up. She encourages her to move with the music.* **DEBRA** *slowly goes with it. For a while the two sisters move together,* **ALEX** *just watches.*)

DEBRA. Dance?

> (**DEBRA** *reaches a hand out to* **ALEX** *over* **GINA**'s *shoulder. He hesitates but gets up, links hands with* **DEBRA**. **GINA** *takes his other hand and the three move round together in an odd unison. It's almost joyful.*)

---

* A licence to produce WHAT'S LOST does not include a performance licence for any third-party or copyrighted music. Licensees should create an original composition or use music in the public domain. For further information, please see Music Use Note on page iii.

(As the music ends they stay together smiling for a moment before separating.)

GINA. Thank you, thanks for that moment

*(**GINA** hangs over, head to the floor.)*

DEBRA. Alright?

GINA. Just grounding my head

DEBRA. Come on. Up.

GINA. Grounding myself

ALEX. I should get off.

DEBRA. You can stay. I can make you up a bed in here.

ALEX. … It's not so late, I'll be fine walking.

DEBRA. If you like.

GINA. Drunk too much.

DEBRA. Go up.

GINA. Can't sleep in that room.

DEBRA. I'll come, join you.

GINA. Really?

DEBRA. Yes. Go on.

*(**GINA** squeezes her hand.)*

Go get ready.

*(**GINA** flings her arms around **ALEX**.)*

GINA. Tomorrow comrade.

*(**GINA** leaves. **ALEX** and **DEBRA** stand looking at each other.)*

ALEX. Had a lot to drink.

DEBRA. Must have needed to.

ALEX. Want it perfect… tomorrow.

(**DEBRA** *moves up very close to him.*)

DEBRA. Stay.

ALEX. …

DEBRA. Stay. Stay.

(She looks at **ALEX**, *she kisses him. She starts to cry, she quickly turns away.* **ALEX** *moves with her, he holds her. He kisses her.)*

(Outside, living room – **GINA** *comes back, with the rolled up canvas in hand, ready to present it. She sees them, withdraws and sits alone with her canvas. She unravels part of it. She listens for a moment to the night. She reassesses the canvas.)*

(Inside, living room – They look at each other. **DEBRA**, *holds his face. He moves away.)*

ALEX. My head…

DEBRA. What's wrong?

(A moment.)

ALEX. It's just I … I might be going away, to work. Don't know, I think. Been looking into… some things. This Human Rights Organisation it, it, practises what it says. Get to work in another country, it's a chance to be somewhere different and they offer all this training for you to develop yourself. Just found out today, it might be possible, it's…

DEBRA. This is your care?

ALEX. No, no, no, no I don't, I don't know what this is so/

DEBRA. Right

ALEX. No. I'm not saying I don't want... I'm just tired. You see it's... Get off the train every morning and where am I? No matter what I planned in my mind, what I try... The journey, the people, step out of the tube and there's someone hustling you. I want to do something, yeah really, but I get in, hear the latest and I know, it could be one of our lot in trouble, has been. Much as we all try, try, try. My energy, it drains. I'm looking for something to bring it up.

Checking the jobs page again. On the internet when I shouldn't be. I'm talking/

DEBRA. It really doesn't matter.

ALEX. I'm just, just trying to explain where I am

DEBRA. I don't care.

(The statement devastates him.)

ALEX. I don't, don't know what this is, that's it/

DEBRA. Stay tonight.

(She stares at him.)

I don't need anything more than that.

11.

An Offering.

(Living room. The next day. **GINA** *enters with the canvas.)*

GINA. Alright?

DEBRA. We've got to go.

GINA. Yeah sorry I've been... How's your head?

DEBRA. Fine.

GINA. After everything... Mine's hanging.

*(***DEBRA** *stops.)*

Okay?

DEBRA. ...

GINA. Dee?

*(***DEBRA** *covers her face with her hands.)*

We can sit

DEBRA. No

*(***DEBRA** *drops her hands and straightens up.)*

GINA. I think we should/

DEBRA. It's fine.

GINA. Take a breath

DEBRA. We've got to move.

GINA. Stop.

DEBRA. I can't stop. *I* can't.

GINA. Can I show you something?

DEBRA. …

GINA. Yes?

DEBRA. We have to go

GINA. It'll take a second. Was thinking of taking it with us I wanted to ask you

> (**GINA** *unravels the canvas, she finds a place to prop it up. It's a stunning collage. All the bits make up a striking picture of* **RUDI**. **DEBRA** *just stares, completely struck by it.*)

An… offering.

> (**DEBRA** *touches it, she doesn't know whether to smile or cry. She looks at* **GINA**.)

Not finished, not completely. But I thought maybe we could have it somewhere there today?

> (**GINA** *waits for her approval.* **DEBRA** *pulls away suddenly, re-gathers her focus.*)

DEBRA. We should go.

> (**DEBRA** *exits.* **GINA** *stares at the collage.*)

12.

No Words.

(The park, alight and alive with candles. Music plays*.)

*(**DEBRA** prepares to address the remembrance crowd. **ALEX** whispers encouragingly and moves off again. The music fades down **DEBRA** moves into position.)*

(She is silent for the longest time...)

DEBRA. ...

...

...

I've no words

(She stops, looks around her. She looks down, up and again around.)

No words.

(She takes in every face.)

There are none...

(She begins to shake.)

What can I show you?

(She decides, she pulls herself up, stares defiantly. She takes out a knife, she carefully places it on her lower arm and cuts herself.)

---

* A licence to produce WHAT'S LOST does not include a performance licence for any third-party or copyrighted music. Licensees should create an original composition or use music in the public domain. For further information, please see Music Use Note on page iii.

It's not real

> *(She cuts herself again.)*

Not real

> *(She cuts again.)*

Not yet

> *(She goes to cut again, **GINA** runs in.)*

GINA. Stop, stop it Dee, stop

> *(**DEBRA**'s hand drops.)*

DEBRA. Not real enough for you is it?

GINA. Dee

> *(**DEBRA** places the knife to cut again. **GINA** moves to take it from her. **DEBRA** holds tight.)*

Please, please Dee, please stop, what are you doing

DEBRA. It's not real enough yet

> *(They struggle until **DEBRA** collapses. **GINA** holds on to her.)*

13.

An Ordinary Family

(The family home, **DEBRA**, **RUDI** *and* **LENNY**, *an ordinary family, moving in and around each other on an ordinary day.* **DEBRA** *stops moving. She watches* **LENNY**. *She moves on to watch* **RUDI** *in her room.* **RUDI** *strums at an instrument or puts some music on and moves round the room to it.** **DEBRA** *watches in awe.)*

---

* A licence to produce WHAT'S LOST does not include a performance licence for any third-party or copyrighted music. Licensees should create an original composition or use music in the public domain. For further information, please see Music Use Note on page iii.

14.

It's Real

(The park. Dark now. The sirens of a police car and ambulance sound. **GINA** *is lit by their flashing lights. She stands alone. News feeds circle...*)*

*(***ALEX** *comes in, his face is wet.)*

ALEX. How could she do that?

GINA. ...

ALEX. I thought she was listening.

GINA. ...

ALEX. Thought she heard.

GINA. ...

ALEX. It's just dumb

GINA. We should've seen, should've seen things weren't right.

ALEX. All we've put into this and she does that

GINA. It's not her fault

ALEX. I have to get out

GINA. Don't go

ALEX. I can't be round all this anymore.

GINA. Wait

ALEX. To do that.

---

*A licence to produce WHAT'S LOST does not include a performance licence for any third-party or copyrighted recordings. Licensees should create their own. Please see note on page iv.

GINA. I didn't see it

ALEX. I can't

>   (**GINA** *takes his hand she squeezes it tight.*)

GINA. She needed help/

ALEX. She let us all down

>   (**GINA** *lets go of his hand.*)

All that time, planning, that's what she had in her head? People get me every time. Sitting there innocent, pretending one thing, then just doing it all their own way.

GINA. She never pretends, we just never saw

ALEX. What can I do if no-one wants it?

I've had enough. I have to get out from here.

>   (**ALEX** *moves quickly away.*)

She let us down, me, and Rudi.

>   (**GINA** *stands alone again. News feeds still circling.* Her mobile rings. She lets it.*)

---

* A licence to produce WHAT'S LOST does not include a performance licence for any third-party or copyrighted recordings. Licensees should create their own. Please see note on page iv.

15.

Chasing Hope

(Hospital room. **DEBRA** *sits up looking ahead.* **GINA** *watches her intently.* **LENNY** *paces.)*

DEBRA. Yes?

(Silence.)

GINA. Don't know what to say to you.

DEBRA. *(Softly.)* Don't speak.

*(***LENNY** *walks up close and stares her out.)*

LENNY. Hurt?

DEBRA. …

LENNY. Hope you do.

DEBRA. Yes.

LENNY. Hope everything's in serious fucking pain.

*(***DEBRA** *stares at him.* **LENNY** *glares back.* **DEBRA** *looks away.* **LENNY** *moves straight back into her eye-line and glares.)*

DEBRA. …

LENNY. …

DEBRA. …

LENNY. Heard on the news, a news report.

Do you know how that is? To have that again?

DEBRA. Yes

LENNY. No, cos you wouldn't have, if you knew.

GINA. Dee

LENNY. Plan it with your little helper?

(Silence.)

What have I done that you shit on me?

DEBRA. I wasn't/

LENNY. Over and over

DEBRA. Just... had to do something.

LENNY. This?

DEBRA. It was something.

LENNY. Public fucking suicide.

DEBRA. It wasn't suicide.

LENNY. No you didn't die.

DEBRA. Wasn't trying to die.

LENNY. Just mutilate yourself?

(DEBRA struggles.)

DEBRA. Thought, I thought... if you witness, the the... mess

LENNY. What?

DEBRA. ... This violence, it's here for something, it's telling us there is something we have to know.

And everyone stops to look, to listen to it/

LENNY. So this is your answer? What d'you want, that recorded?

Shown in schools?

DEBRA. You can't judge

LENNY. You need help.

DEBRA. Who are you... who are you to judge. I tried to do something. What did you do?

LENNY. What, cos I didn't go out and crush him, crush his family? Cos I'm not giant enough to help the people I love?

DEBRA. You wouldn't talk

LENNY. What is there to say?

DEBRA. Anything

GINA. I got to… get air.

> (**GINA** *walks out of the room and outside the hospital. She kicks out, at anything in her way.*)
>
> (*Inside –* **LENNY** *just stares at* **DEBRA**.)
>
> (*Outside –* **GINA** *takes out a cigarette, considers.*)
>
> (*Inside –* **DEBRA** *turns away from* **LENNY**.)

LENNY. What should I do?

Rip my insides out and show you how screwed they are? Or my mind, my heart? If there's anything there. Cos I tell you Dee, there's so little, I'm disintegrating.

DEBRA. Disintegrating's easy.

LENNY. It's fucking not. It's not.

DEBRA. *(Intensely.)* I thought we had life. Thought it was all going somewhere, escalating to something.

I work hard, that's what I was brought up with. And I shouldn't be here. Shouldn't have to be here.

LENNY. No one should.

DEBRA. Why did she have to get involved?

LENNY. You can't keep going over it.

> (*A moment.*)

DEBRA. What's brought me this? I shouldn't have it.

Might as well have stayed where we were/

LENNY. Hold on/

DEBRA. Moved further east.

LENNY. So it's me? My fault?

DEBRA. ... No. No.

> *(Outside –* **GINA** *lights up, she takes a few useless puffs.)*
>
> *(Inside –* **DEBRA** *struggles.)*

Thought I was doing things right.

Had her. Gave love, even when I ...just wanted to squash her, and sometimes I did.

LENNY. Don't

DEBRA. Gave love even when she was awkward and selfish/

LENNY. Don't start that

DEBRA. Is it thinking the wrong thoughts? Did I attract this?

> *(Outside –* **GINA** *wipes her eyes. She watches the smoke dissolve in the air.)*
>
> *(Inside –* **LENNY** *goes and rests his head against* **DEBRA***'s. She sinks a bit. They stay just like that for a long time.)*

Should have gone round the world.

LENNY. Maybe you should've.

> *(***LENNY** *starts to leave.)*

DEBRA. It's just, what it could have been... I miss that.

> *(***LENNY** *stops.)*

LENNY. I know. But we've got to deal with what's now.

DEBRA. How?

LENNY. …

DEBRA. …

LENNY. Rest. I'll be here, whenever.

> *(He walks out.)*
>
> *(Outside –* **LENNY** *stops by* **GINA**. *She takes his hand. They don't talk, just hold hands tight for a moment.* **GINA** *kisses his hand, moves back to the room.)*
>
> *(Inside –* **DEBRA** *tries to stand as* **GINA** *enters.)*

GINA. What you doing?

DEBRA. Can't lie here, I'm not the victim.

GINA. You're not fit.

Won't just let you go.

DEBRA. …

GINA. Police want to talk to you.

DEBRA. They would.

GINA. And you need to see a doctor

DEBRA. … What happened to Alex?

GINA. He's gone. He was upset.

DEBRA. Everyone's upset with me.

GINA. You hurt him

DEBRA. … Child.

> *(Silence.)*

GINA. Don't get you. Don't get this. Usually me.

I'm the one that/

DEBRA. Was thinking of you. What you would go for.

GINA. This?

DEBRA. Something... big.

GINA. Never this.

Still so many possibilities. I doubt, of course I doubt. Spent so much time pushing in one direction. Wonder if I've wasted myself but I have to see it out

DEBRA. It's not about you

GINA. No

DEBRA. Not everything's you

GINA. I know that, I know

DEBRA. Then stop, stop, just stop.

(A moment.)

GINA. You can't give in. That's all I wanted to say.

DEBRA. ...

GINA. And I'm here.

DEBRA. How long?

GINA. As long as

DEBRA. Because you have nowhere else.

GINA. ... I should've looked after you. Should've

(**DEBRA** *looks at her.*)

DEBRA. I can do that.

GINA. No you can't.

DEBRA. I have, and I will

GINA. Don't want me?

DEBRA. I don't want to fight.

GINA. ...

DEBRA. Even the silent in your head arguments we have.

GINA. You, never me.

DEBRA. No, you just say it, whatever it is.

GINA. Alright.

(They half smile at each other.)

DEBRA. ... I think this is my punishment. For not doing what I should have. For betraying something I should have been.

GINA. No such thing.

DEBRA. But there was. Should I have married Lenny?

GINA. Come on/

DEBRA. Moved here. Avoided involvement in all the things I was supposed to have been.

GINA. We both did.

DEBRA. And who's having a greater life for it?

GINA. You're not to blame Dee

DEBRA. It's stepped in. Those two little black girls from Forest Gate are pulling, pulling me back.

GINA. What's that mean?

DEBRA. That's what we were growing up. And everywhere we looked we saw what that meant. Black was second to white, working for wasn't as good as already owning. We pushed to prove, to get away... I pushed... but where am I?

GINA. Here.

DEBRA. Still labelled.

GINA. We're here, doing what we want.

DEBRA. What do people think when they see my story?

GINA. They can think what they like.

(Silence.)

DEBRA. ... Built up this world me Lenny... Rudi. That was something, that was my something but, where am I now?

GINA. Know you never listen to me, know you think I'm the idiot that always proves you right, but that's wrong. We've done things, we've moved on, we've been who we are and we're here, Rudi was here. She's in everything. She was seventeen with the mind of a forty-year-old. She was beautiful and intelligent, fearless.

DEBRA *stands up.*

DEBRA. Past is calling for more.

GINA. Rudi was here and, she inspires me.

(Silence.)

DEBRA. Your picture, offering. It's beautiful. It's something.

GINA. ... That means so much

DEBRA. I saw what you're all about in it.

(They stare at each other.)

Hate what's in my head sometimes, the bitterness, this fury. That is someone I never wanted to be. And somehow I can't stop the thoughts, it's... exploding from me.

I'm exploding.

GINA. Relax Dee.

DEBRA. I can't believe how long I've worn this face.

GINA. You've got to relax yourself now.

(Silence.)

DEBRA. How do I look?

GINA. Alright.

DEBRA. Liar.

>   (**GINA** *looks away.*)

My hair could do with a style.

Any advice?

*(***GINA** *doesn't respond.)*

DEBRA. Might get locks.

GINA. Suit you.

DEBRA. Like to leave the world with locks on my head. Maybe when I'm fifty, sixty.

GINA. It'd really suit you.

>   (**GINA** *looks back at her, sees her small on the bed.*)

Your... skin's all dry

DEBRA. ...

>   (**GINA** *searches her bag, She gets out her hand cream. She hesitates.*)

GINA. Can I?

>   (**DEBRA** *shrugs.* **GINA** *silently squeezes the tube and very softly rubs cream into* **DEBRA***'s arms.* **DEBRA** *lets her. When she's finished* **GINA** *climbs on the bed next to her.*)

Last time we slept in the same bed I think I was, seven?

DEBRA. ... Sorry.

GINA. No/

DEBRA. I am. I just wanted some meaning. Some sense.

Justice…

Something.

GINA. I should have been here. Just couldn't, couldn't face it. Me…

I'm the one to be sorry.

DEBRA. … The day after… Day we spoke I went for a drink. Wanted to be alone in company, somewhere comforting. So I went to a proper old, Romford road-style pub. One I'd avoid usually, normally. Sat with this bottle of wine, waiting for some sort of comfort to kick in. It wasn't the kind of place you buy a bottle of wine, so I think everyone understood to leave me. Something about the place reminded me of us. You, me, mum, dad. Our own little unit. All they used to do with us, how much of each other's life we were. Some of their best times were with us, what are our best times now? What are mine? I wanted them back… There were these two women, in their eighties I think. Sat across the other side drinking. Looked like they'd been there for decades. They had completely made-up faces. Eye-shadow, rouged cheeks, bright plum lips. Like teenagers when they first start… They looked like good mates. One, her eyes just closed and her head fell, right there. I sat staring, waiting for her head to come up again. Sat there thinking…

All this time… I'd been this person, this rigid, rigid mother person, there was no time to be anything else, no time for things to develop between us. I missed what we could have been. Watched these two thinking that.

The friend got up and walked out. I drained this bottle, watching this woman for signs of breath. I started getting… irate, you can't just leave people. You can't. You can't just leave them… Rudi knew that, that's why she jumped in to help like she did. She was being the person we wanted her to be.

And I really miss her.

16.

What's Lost

*(**RUDI**'s room. **GINA** and **RUDI** as they were at the beginning.)*

RUDI. Next week. By the sea.

GINA. Be nice, be great to have you there, some point

RUDI. We can paddle. Feel the coldness of night beneath our feet. The shock of it.

Nice sometimes to be shocked into feeling.

GINA. I've… lots on at the moment, tons of work possibilities. I'm looking into this new idea, the flat's a mess with it

RUDI. Not expecting five star

GINA. Plan it for when things are a bit more sorted out, okay.

*(**RUDI** just looks at her.)*

RUDI. Mum said

GINA. What?

RUDI. Said you've… lots to get sorted.

(A moment.)

It'll be fine. It will be.

GINA. Yeah.

RUDI. No. It will, don't worry.

(**RUDI** *plays some music.**)

What d'you think of this one?

(They listen. **GINA** *nods approval.)*

GINA. Yeah, nice.

RUDI. ... I think, all your work, your time your... love. It's good, it's for something good. That's what makes it worth doing, you know you're trying to really do something in the world? It'll be fine.

(**GINA** *smiles.*)

If not now maybe once you've gone.

GINA. Right.

RUDI. You'll be revived.

Everything good's revived, eventually.

GINA. Really.

RUDI. And some crap too.

(**GINA** *laughs.*)

I mean it. It's great what you do.

Hope I can stand for something.

Nothing matters more.

GINA. You're very, very... cool.

RUDI. I'll come whenever you're ready. We can work on something maybe, something... significant?

Might help if we do it together.

---

* A licence to produce WHAT'S LOST does not include a performance licence for any third-party or copyrighted music. Licensees should create an original composition or use music in the public domain. For further information, please see Music Use Note on page iii.

*(**GINA** thinks about it. She smiles. She moves away.)*

*(She takes a deep breath and moves to **DEBRA**.)*

(The night gets a little brighter.)

ABOUT THE AUTHOR

Paula B Stanic grew up in Manor Park, East London. She's a winner of the Alfred Fagon Award and the Adrienne Benham Award. She's been a writer in residence (Soho Theatre) & writer on attachment (NT Studio). She was part of the 2016/17 Drama Room (BBC Writersroom) and on the BBC New Talent Hotlist. Her plays include: *Monday* (Red Ladder) short-listed for the John Whiting Award; *Pancras Boys Club* co-written with Ben Musgrave and David Watson (Only Connect); *6 Minutes 'Everything Must Go'* (Soho Theatre); *Under a Foreign Sky* (Theatre Centre); *Steering Through Stars* (Tangle) and *Miss World... 1970* (Peer Productions). She was recently co-writer on *Messiah* with Jesse Briton (National tour).

www.ingramcontent.com/pod-product-compliance
Ingram Content Group UK Ltd.
Pitfield, Milton Keynes, MK11 3LW, UK
UKHW021839210426
5322IPUK00022B/377